SOULS

Moniza Alvi was born in Pakistan and grew up in Hertfordshire. She was co-winner of The Poetry Business Prize in 1991. Her first collection *The Country at My Shoulder* (OUP, 1993) was shortlisted for the T.S. Eliot and Whitbread poetry prizes, and was selected for the New Generation Poets promotion. *A Bowl of Warm Air* (OUP, 1996) was featured in *The Independent on Sunday*'s 'Books of the Year'. *Carrying My Wife* (Bloodaxe Books, 2000) was a Poetry Book Society Recommendation. Her latest collection is *Souls* (Bloodaxe Books, 2002).

Her third collection, *Carrying My Wife* is published in an edition which also includes *The Country at My Shoulder* and *A Bowl of Warm Air*. She reads poems from all three collections on *The Poetry Quartets 6* (The British Council/Bloodaxe Books, 2000), a double-cassette shared with Michael Donaghy, Anne Stevenson and George Szirtes.

After a long career as a secondary school teacher, she now lives in south west London with her husband and young daughter. She is a tutor for the Open College of the Arts and the Poetry School.

MONIZA ALVI

SOULS

To Jane
warm wishes
Moniza Alvi

BLOODAXE BOOKS

Copyright © Moniza Alvi 2002

ISBN: 1 85224 585 9

First published 2002 by
Bloodaxe Books Ltd,
Highgreen,
Tarset,
Northumberland NE48 1RP.

www.bloodaxebooks.com
For further information about Bloodaxe titles
please visit our website or write to
the above address for a catalogue.

Bloodaxe Books Ltd acknowledges
the financial assistance of Northern Arts.

Cover printing by J. Thomson Colour Printers Ltd, Glasgow.

Printed in Great Britain by
Cromwell Press Ltd, Trowbridge, Wiltshire.

for Jenny, Jane and Rose

Acknowledgements

Acknowledgements are due to the editors of the following publications in which some of these poems first appeared: *Making Worlds* (Headland Books, 2001), *Poetry London, PN Review, Poetry Review, Poetry Wales, The Journal of Literature and Aesthetics* (India), *The Rialto* and *The Waterlog*.

'Of Chairs and Shadows' was commissioned by the artist Eileen Hogan.

For the poem 'Immortals', I am indebted to an article by A.C. Grayling in *The Guardian*.

The quotation on page 39 is taken from Fernando Pessoa's 'If, after I die, they want to write my biography', from *Poems of Fernando Pessoa*, translated by Edwin Honig and Susan M. Brown (City Lights Books).

Contents

*

THE FURTHER ADVENTURES
OF THE SOULS

Presents

Come closer.
It is Christmas morning.

The souls are opening their presents,
unpacking their empty boxes
in perfect harmony with the void.

Nothingness is the most sensible gift –
it doesn't clash with anything
and if you have some already
it isn't a problem to receive a little more.

The souls hold it shakily on a spoon
as if they are ravenous
as if they are about to eat.

Don't Pity Them

They bring their own daylight
which they transport, folded

in soft white tissue paper.
Souls are renowned collectors –

they wait like indoor birdwatchers
in hallways and doorways

for lozenges of light.
Create your own world,

they advise. *Collect nothing
which isn't infinitely collectible.*

Don't pity them
as they bend over their scrapbooks,

cutting and sticking, rearranging the light.

Whatever the Weather

It's essential that the souls
don't make themselves too obvious.
Think what might happen
if they revealed themselves openly –
they'd be blamed for everything.

So they ensure they're harder
to contemplate
than summer in winter.
Whatever the weather,
how discreet they are!

Young souls learn to dress themselves –
wrap themselves in obscurity.

The Scene of the Crime

The set – a country house
with oak panelling, and outside

a blizzard from a melodrama.
An inspector called to investigate

the disappearance of a soul –
a murder by an unseen hand.

The souls – are they ever he or she?
Hot or cold? Who knows.

Perhaps, when they go
they're inquisitive, as curious

as those who seek them?
Do they leave alone, or could they

huddle together behind a sofa
in a snowbound manor?

There's not a single clue.
Just polite conversation growing

steadily more frenzied.
A door slams, dislodging

a lampshade. And somewhere
out in the night,

a soul goes off like a gun.

Without Us

Souls are divorced many times
They exist as discarded fragments –
a name left behind,

an unfashionable scarf,
nail parings.
They are so light without us.

They survive alone
like bedsit dwellers
very close to their own atmosphere.

They can cope with this.
But a room is uneasy
with an invisible occupant.

    The landlady catches her breath
    and pulls her chair closer to the fire.

Travellers

Generally, they're good travellers,
well equipped – life's experiences
stuffed into their airy rucksacks.
The souls love skimming the tops of trees.
Though some flutter noisily,
protesting like bored children
Are we nearly there yet?

And what can the world do,
but put its hands over its ears?

Lost Souls

Lost souls are not always lost.
They inhabit us as if our faces
were portraits in galleries –

and stare out of us
until they are tired of looking.
We are tired too – boxed in,
exhausted with sitting still.
Eventually we get cramp,
backache, however sumptuous
our clothes, rosy our cheeks.

Strangely, when the souls
are tired of looking,
it does sometimes happen
that our clothes rustle,
our eyes move.

Who Can Blame Them?

And some are forced to grow
as fast as possible –
let's call them chicken souls.

Crammed into sheds
or shackled upside down,
they develop abnormalities.
Who can blame them
when they peck at painkillers,
or envy those allowed

to go outside –
though rumour has it
all that fresh air's rationed
and the frost
puts hostile feathers
on the backs of chicken souls.

Bat

Like a bat it hangs, and keeps on hanging.
Hibernating – or in need of help?
The soul is a vulnerable species –
and some get very worn, as bats
might have worn teeth.

The soul, hanging on out there,
on a wall, longing
to fit into the palm of a hand.

Immortals

The souls are continually hunting
fervent as hounds, not for a fox,
but for a den – somewhere
to lie down, set up home.

We feel for them,
because who would wish
to live forever?

But they're bemused –
we live our lives,
tell our stories,
ignorant of the last instalment.

We only know about life.
To the souls,
we're the real immortals.

In Space

When souls go into orbit
they find the food impossible –

bite-sized cubes, zero-gravity meals
and everything heat-treated
to prevent decay. Scissors
for snipping the tops off food bags –
the souls float straight through them.

They evade it all
and make for deeper space,
vow to consume nothing
but songs without words.

They mock us gently –
our brief space flights,
the music we try to clothe
with flesh and bone.

The Worst Thing

The worst thing for the souls
is forgetting how to fly.

No chance to star
on Prospero's island.

They'll almost grieve,
then lie in wait

for the moment of their
liberation –

when even the most inept
will soar so high and fast

no sharp-eared god
can hear them coming.

The Marriage

They get used to crowds,
huge, seething crowds,
surging down the streets
and across the fields,
filling the crevices.

No space between the blades of grass.
Not just crowds of themselves,
the multiplicity of souls –
but throngs of hopes and desires,

fateful endeavours,
joys, perplexities,
do's and don'ts.

The souls marry the crowds.
There's no ceremony,
though sometimes there's music,
muffled, cacophonous –
and the bells of lost churches

ring out under the sea.

The Other Room

This is the room reflected in the window.
Walk inside, explore it for yourself.
The fire is glacial crimson.

The walls are filmy, not like walls at all.
These are the most densely populated
living-rooms on earth.

But who lives in them? The souls
settle here in their multitudes,
visit the spines of weightless books,

the floating hands of clocks.
Sink into armchairs in the snow.
Lose interest in us, even

as they beat so fiercely
against our bolder rooms,
the glass of the world.

Beds

They can't decide whether finally
they are more, or less alone,

and can't help longing
for a real, solid bed,

pine, or four-poster, to share
with one other soul –

not the thousands
who'd attempt to drift in.

What do the souls do in bed?
Not touching exactly,

but a warm overlapping.
In the morning they descend

the stairs, separate from the world
but only slightly

like a girl who has just
washed her hair, and they

assure themselves that after all
they are a marvellous invention.

Family Reunions

Just when they think they've made it –
the shock
of numberless, faceless relatives
filling up infinity.

Awkward meetings.
Parties with invisible food and drink.
Embarrassed shiftings
take the place of dancing.

Family reunions are overwhelming
for the souls.
The semi-familiar billions.
No getaway car.

Nowhere else to go.

Escape

The souls are playing truant,
escaping the strain of us,
finding places to hide –

in lifts and murky stairwells,
under bridges. Up there
with the pigeons, they glance

down and marvel at
how hard we try to tell one
soul from another, the boxes

we force them in, the countries
we try to pin on them.
But they won't have it.

However hard we press down
on the lid, out they come,
out of the box.

The Directors

They're busiest at night,
fiddling with the roots of our hair,
stroking the backs of our eyes,
setting in motion the nightly film.

As the dream gathers its singular
momentum, the souls burrow
into our bones, circle
just above our heads...

Then one night the dream slips
away from them, fizzles out.
So what can they do when
we've skidded into their past?

The directors of nothing.
Did we give up on them,
or them on us?

Shirt on the Line

The souls are not always serious.
It is such fun for them
to inhabit the shirt on the line.

The white shirt, usually so proper –
tucked in and belted into place.
The soul, like the wind

fills out the chest,
and the sleeves are riotous,
swaying and flapping.

The empty shirt is a joy –
for an hour the souls forget
what they carry with them,

have no idea whether
it is a happy childhood,
or a great weariness.

A Soul is Showing

Sometimes a soul is showing.

You can glimpse it like a slip
hanging an inch below a skirt.

You see it,
      then your friend sees it,
            your neighbour,
the man at the corner shop.

And even those at a great distance
seem to perceive it –

the lighthouse keeper,
so used to the souls
repeating themselves
on the tips of waves.

Perhaps it's not such a big deal.
No need to be embarrassed
because a soul is showing.

Quiet Work

So much time spent
hovering inside us, uncomplainingly.
Their quiet work is never done –

the slow linking of our past's past
to our future's future
with no elaborate equipment.

How different the souls are
from the beleaguered memory,
stalking through a lost empire,

excited about the catch of the day,
fingering the stolen goods.

Even the Sun

Expanding souls shoot upwards, outwards,
persuade us to extend their homes,
make balconies, rooms in the roof,
more space for guests.
To them, so much is possible –

even the moon could call them up,
even the sun could stay the night.

Great and Small

The second is the great thing,
not the years, the days,
the protracted minutes.
The souls know so well
the particles of time,
their scent,
their explosive nature.

If there's a special vibrancy,
or a stillness in the air,
it could be the souls
protecting the seconds,
feeding them, patting them.

Perhaps it's our final second,
and the souls are attentive, fixed
on that small living thing.

Something Like

And so the souls came to live
in a country where everything
was something like something else
and nothing was the thing itself.

The sun, for instance
was like a melon someone
had broken open and
put back together again
awkwardly.

And face-like shapes
appeared on a vast scale, but faintly,
as if paint had been applied
to a canvas with something like a sponge.

> At a time resembling afternoon,
> someone like you
> could have a kind of tea
> with someone who was almost
> a person.

The life of the soul, was it life
itself, or something approximating to it?
At times, it was encouragingly like it.

Strangers

Each soul is a stranger to the other,
as if one were a trapeze artist
and another a refuse collector,
or a museum attendant.
But each contains a definite hint
of the other, as if the trapeze artist
could easily take on the glance
of the refuse collector.
Each soul in its separate guise
passes down the thoroughfare.

When the souls collide,
they are confused because
they cannot easily tell whether
it is themselves or the other
who is the museum attendant.
Some linger on street corners
trying to work it out
with a fine degree of patience –
the customs of the infinite,
and the weather permitting.

The Inspection

Of course, you cannot look at a soul
under a magnifying glass,

but it's tempting to try.
To hold one securely between
your finger and thumb,
taking care not to pinch it.

Lay it on a sheet,
or table-top, and capture it
in an instant when it isn't
folding in on itself.

Suppose the soul's a kind of cloud
somewhere between hyacinth
and grape green, with a rind
like a slice of lemon...

Then suddenly there's no thick lens.
Just your open eyes –
and your peopled life
rising up, as if for an inspection.

And melting quickly away.

Hotel

All those passages and corridors,
deep red walls and indoor rivers.

So what does the soul
think of its temporary home,
the spongy,
        the leaky places
and the heart, like Big Ben
presiding over everything?

Perhaps the soul is drawn
to the body's holes and windows,
knowing that one day
it will surely leave.
Without a backward glance.

Was the body really such a good hotel?

Without Them

The souls often wonder
what we'd be like
without them,
if we'd be able to carry on.

Perhaps we'd invite something else in –
a spool of magnetic tape.
Gravel.
A black sun.

They picture us on the road,
desperate for a lift,
a snack from another planet.
The soulless – stricken like scarecrows.

Intent on startling the seasons away.

Two Dates

There are only two dates: my day of birth, day of death.
FERNANDO PESSOA

Through all our frenetic years
they have no real need for diaries.

The souls carry with them
our first stupendous day –
and leave a space for our unknown last.

Two dates which bind together
our existence.

As soon as they have them both
they'll throw them to the heavens
like confetti.

Ridding themselves of clutter.
Unravelling all our days.

Do They Miss Us?

Eventually, they do.

Not our bodies,
the intricate workings,
the fine limbs – not our minds,
nor even our hearts. Not really
us, but themselves in us –

the souls wriggling into place.
A flame in a gemstone.
A live wire. Truly
we were the great love
of their unfathomable lives.

The Scanner

Who could bear to look at their own soul?
Who could contain their excitement?
Better by far, with a semblance of calm,
to point the scanner at someone else
in the hope of a unique sighting.

Not everyone approves.
And there have been complaints
even from the souls themselves
who beg to be left alone
to do their own thing.

Blameless souls,
swimming in the depths of simplicity!

This Town

This town we think is home,
is somewhere else. Abroad.
Every night we travel
miles and miles to get here,

and if, in the morning, it seems
familiar, that's just
a trick of the light. It isn't
our bedroom, our bedclothes.

Even our breath is scarcely
our own – the souls maintain
they gave it as a gift.
Quite casually.

How did they come to let it go?
Doubtful, we shake our heads.

Delight

Days that we perceive the least
because they flow so fast –

rare days that run like rivers.
The souls wade in, and splash about.

Out There

Most days, the souls
would rather be somewhere else.

Not bottled up,
but out there in a landscape,
under an old oak, by a wood signposted
private, watching the bushes
grow pricklier, wilder, adding
their little bit of transfiguration,
like a shaft of sun through cloud.
Not proprietorial, lordly
in the foreground, like Gainsborough's
Mr and Mrs Andrews,
but merging into the fields –
as one brushstroke disappears into the next.

Ventriloquism

They can't sit us on their knee.
Though when the act is over
it's just as if we're stuffed into a suitcase.

And what about those insinuations?
The repartee from nowhere?
Someone is calling you personally,

from within, from the corner of the room.
Then voices everywhere – in the cellar,
up on the roof.

The souls are determined – practising
ventriloquism as if they had
a larynx, a throat.

More intriguing than the radio,
the telephone – this oracle,
this ceaseless voice.

Yes

Soul mates explode with *yes* –
it isn't a word,
but a gust of air, a volley of light.

They are their own children,
their own parents.
And where is *no*,
that wastrel *no*?

They have taken him
out into the woods
and left him there.

Lovers

Fortunate souls have countless lovers.
The silver birches love them.

The fat sizzling in the pan.
The alphabet loves them, even the rarer letters,

and the vacancies between words.
The heroic titles of books love them.

The doorknobs and switches.
The paint thinner, the smear of apricot jam.

And the bubble harbours rainbow lights
for them and swells like a soul itself,

adored, buoyant, doomed to reach
perfection – just before it bursts.

When We're Very Still

Occasionally, when we're very still,
the souls take fright
and think we've died, anticipate
the loss of a partner.
Like people posing for a photograph,
we're still, before we're stilled.

When we really die, some souls
are traumatised,
and take to drink – those liquids
offered by another world.
So dry they could be
manufactured in the desert.

Back on earth
there's someone missing.

Yet there's so much life
a soul could drown in it.

Trapped

A soul has a horror
of being trapped underground.
So, experimentally
it prepares itself, inhabits
a loaf of bread,
the heart of a stone.

But it can't prepare itself
for the totality – the relentlessness
of soil, the maggots and the grit.
The way, at last, the world
appears, but darker, stuffier –
a subterranean department store.

No windows, no natural light at all.
Caverns, grottos, useless things for sale.

Nothing

'Bring nothing with you' the notice says.
And dutifully the souls shed everything.

But desperately
they gather up nothing and hold it

close to them, as if it were a child.
Nothing is more precious than life,

the souls chant. *Let's dance.*
And then the music stops.

And then they lose their voice.

Eine Kleine Nachtmusik

(after the painting by Dorothea Tanning)

You can lock the doors, even
bolt the air, but there's no way
of keeping your daughters in at night.
It doesn't matter how old they are –
three or four, six or seven –
a tornado throws them down the path
and ravishes them.
Stars glint like metal in their hair.
The darkness, fine as artists' ink,
seeps into their nightclothes.
If you follow them down the path –
you turn to stone.

Then long after the midnight hour
the wind flings them back into the hallway
and up onto the landing
with its cracked green paint.
Their blouses open up like curtains
on their narrow, childish chests.

Your daughters grow giant sunflowers
in the gloom.
Their hair streams upwards
thick as cypress trees.

The Conjurors

How could they have known
that their child would finally arrive
so much more impressively
than a rabbit from a hat,
and then keep on arriving
like the silk scarves
knotted into an endless rope.

Experimentally, playfully
the conjuror-parents had lifted up
their own lives and covered them
with a soft, red cloth, and those
lives had duly vanished,
never to reappear
in the same form, despite

the most theatrical of gestures,
the most solemn incantations.

Her Parents Are Lonely

after all, there are only two of them
on the whole wide earth.
Surely their infant
who is so many weathers,
must have a multitude of parents –

so her mother and father scanned
the horizon searching for the others,
the lost parents of their child.
Perhaps they would drift
across the hills in pairs
at first slowly, then eagerly,

as if glad to have left the ark
and found themselves on dry land.

The Twins

And so the twins were born –
not two infants
but a mother and a father.

Clearly they were not identical,
and they were not inseparable.
But suddenly they shared a birth-time
though they couldn't tell
whether they were years old
or just a second old.

      Often their child filled entirely
      their watchful compound eye.

      Their hands were continually busy
      making a sinewy cat's cradle.
      At times their fingers moved
      in sympathy as if one pair of hands
      was sketching the other.

      And these twins tried to wear
      the same clothes – flecked
      with their shaky authority.

In their darkest hours
they were afraid of falling
through the galaxy,
of snapping apart
at their shiny hinge.

      They were two moons
               two suns
                    two trees
      bending over a hammock.
      They were lighter, heavier
      than they'd ever been,
      more hollow and more solid.

And still their single lives continued
like the remnants of a festival
in another town.

The Captain's Child

She moved as if within a circle of sea-air.
Then she stepped outside this private zone
and held it, shrunk small and watery
like a bubble in her hands.

Inside this sphere was a tiny ship
so dazzling, so covered in reflections
its surfaces were hardly visible at all.
She was the captain's child –

and the captain of her ship.

Island Daughter

She plays quietly on the island,
frightened to wake the babies.
A century ago she was an infant herself –

now she's older than her parents.
They watch with her for the signal –
the shooting light in the trees.

Once the sea is certain of her name
she'll leave stealthily
on a raft heaped with everything

she thinks she'll never need,
the sail lashed tightly
to the mast of her childhood.

Turbines

In the end
we were nothing more

and nothing less
than two wind turbines

masking the view,
while our children tore,

shouting, across the wavy
lines of the hills.

We were massive,
the largest in the land.

Starkly visible, we strode
into the sky – then

off the stage completely,
holding in our arms

that rush of air
we tried

to make our own.

Go Back to England

Model Town, Lahore.
I was born there, lived there

briefly.
What was it like?

Nothing like the houses I built
from Lego. Not a bit like

Welwyn Garden City.
But perhaps the houses *were*

spaced out and the gardens tended.
Lemon trees. Not apple trees.

*

In Model Town, the story goes,
to save money,

my mother made my father's
handkerchiefs from his shirt tails.

My mother, newly married
and wrapped in her Englishness,

tried to make herself at home
in her husband's Pakistan.

Cycled along the sweltering lane
to play Mrs Plover's piano.

Sometimes, at night,
the buffaloes wandered in

and grazed on the lawn.
What a noise they made!

She hardly missed Hatfield at all.

*

At least, not until 1954.
What happened then?

Well, I was born –
and the seismic happening

the birth of a child, rocked
everything.

The flat-roofed house trembled,
the grey-green trees shook,

and the ground beneath
my mother's feet gaped.

Kicking above the cracks
was a baby, who wailed,

who detested the heat
and the cold.

It was as if the solid house
had collapsed.

But the earth couldn't swallow up
the baby clinics

because there weren't any,
couldn't swallow up the wise advice

because there wasn't any.
And where was a set of scales

to weigh a baby?

*

So there was my mother – suddenly
thousands of miles from home.

Her phrase book instructed
You must water the plants

while I am away in the hills.
But that was no use at all.

And the lemon trees
were no use at all.

*

Go back to England
said the doctor.

Go back to England
said the stones and boulders.

Go back to England
urged the dusty grass.

*

July gasped in the heat
the day we left Model Town.

My mother hoped to be
a different mother.

The ocean knew
I would be translated

into an English girl.

Model Town: a district of Lahore.

The House with One Window

Things that are too wintry –
like a hole dug in a frozen garden
and darkness falling.
A house with one window.
A smile with the mouth
and not with the eyes.
The muffling of the soul.
Things I shouldn't write about
that dissolve like snowmen
in the rain

*

A first brother –
younger than me.
Eternally young.
And suddenly
I'm in the little house
with one window.

*

I asked
Where is he?
And the answer swooped in –
He's gone on a journey.
Everything in the room
moved fractionally
as if it had gone
on a journey too.
But I couldn't go.
Perhaps because the way was too icy
or too far
like over a mountain range.
Or too adventurous.
Another world.

In this movement
of everything
I was very still.

*

I'd raced across the ward
to visit him –
the lino was so shiny
and slippery I fell.
I'd been walking a year
and it was as if I'd run my first race
on this burnished floor
brown as a conker
wide as a river.
And the cots were there
on the other side –
the bank
just out of reach.
I fell in, my eagerness
swallowed up.
I could have been an adult
feeling shame
at losing control.

The sick-ward had no windows at all.

*

Absence was
an arm where there was no arm
an eye with no colour
no reflections
a smile but no mouth.
And the house more spacious –

no brother.

In a way it was a golden space.
Presence and absence
tried to sit down
and play by the fire.

*

Scarcely more
than a baby myself
I held a baby
inside me
as a camera

might hold inside it
the ghost
of a photograph
or a feather might whisper
the idea of a bird
or a soul might receive
the imprint
of a soul.

*

Hatted and mittened
I am peering into
his Rolls-Royce pram.
His face is broad
as health.
He's wide-mouthed
as if he's smiling
gazing out of the photograph
into my parents' tidied
bedroom –
into the airy
the airless
distance.

*

So what's left?
The bleak force of it all.
And a curious feeling
of balance –
those inner scales.
Sorrow, the exact weight
of love.
Our children
our parents
on loan like library books.

A house with one window
opening, closing, shuttered, opening

The Bells

The streets are well-lit at the heart of the child.
He hasn't seen them yet –
but there are elegant, gracious squares,
shady trees and fountains.
The inhabitants are certain where to go
and newcomers are carefully questioned.

Streets away, at the edge of the suburbs
the lights start to dim
and the trees along the avenues agitate.
People scurry about in confusion
and the roads disappear altogether.
Buildings are ramshackle,
haunted by the derelicts, the isolates.
They have no official papers.

But still the bells ring out
in the elegant squares,
tremendous peals
more than the ear can cope with –
ring out in the heads of the most
unsettling of strangers.

The huge bells of adulthood

The huge bells of childhood

The Boy from Bombay
(for Varuna and Jan)

He sleeps – one fist clenched
on a fragment of India.

Shadow-brothers
moving behind his eyelids
curl up on their low beds
clatter their metal breakfast plates.
A roomful of lost boys.

He wakes to the crisp Swiss air
the clean grey streets
a view of the mountains.
He wakes to new parents.
At last they'd brought him home!

*

The new child with the new name.
Amit André, seeing with his ears
hearing with his eyes,
his present tumbling
over his past and future.
An absence of dust.

A computerised image
of Amit with elephants
announces his arrival.
His forefinger stroking
an immense turquoise forehead.
The boy from Bombay
in loving command
of paper animals.
His eyes watchful
and amazed.

*

Years later, perhaps,
he'll look in the mirror
and picture himself
for a moment
somewhere else.

Not in this town numbed
by snow, but under the yellow
basalt of the Gateway of India.
Or buying pomfret in the market.

*

He strains to see –
as if he could uncover
the full story.
As if he could untie
a boat on the lake,
row it from one world
to another –

backwards and forwards –
through the sunlight
and the shadows.

Flight

What is it about Mohammed Ayaz
that sticks in the mind?

Is it how he squeezed himself
into the wheel bay
    of a Boeing 777,
found somewhere to crouch and cling?

Is it how, at 30,000 ft in the freezing
dark, he turned into a block of ice?

Is it where his twisted body was found,
in a DIY store car park,
    in London,
by a worker – on her way
to load paint tins
    into strong paper bags?

What is it about Mohammed Ayaz
that sticks in the mind?

Is it his foolishness?
Is it his courage?

Is it that his family's debts,
were as high as Mount Mankial?

    Harvesting the onion crop,
        they had so little time to grieve.

Is it that 3,000 people share
only one telephone
in the broad green valley of Swat?

Is it that routinely the captain
opened the undercarriage
and tipped him out?

    And others will fall in this way,
        on almost exactly the same spot.

Allah gives and Allah takes away
said his father.
He was meant to die
at this time.

But the son who had fallen
to earth groaned
It was the wrong time.
The wrong way.

The Tunnel

I was stunned, as anyone would be
to find themselves metamorphosed
into a tunnel, that someone
wanted to get through – but
they couldn't just amble along
or drive straight to the end.

Perspectives were lost.
No daylight could be glimpsed
though red flowers
dripped from the ceiling.

It was part of the earth
but the floor was tender –
you'd have to walk barefoot.
It was very close, very damp.
A passage under the sea,
through the mountains.
And pain chiselling away
with his astonishing tool kit,
his axes and wrenches,
his screwdrivers and his knives.
Busier and busier.

I would have spoken
with my echoey voice.
Calmed the one inside
who was trying to escape
almost against her will.

Sleep, I would say.
Sleep and try again.
The world is waiting.

Enormous

How could it have happened
that she had given birth
to a baby so much bigger than herself?

    She could hardly lift him –
    dragged him onto her bed.

She was the helpless one.
Well-meant words
shrivelled in the air.
Visitors smiled uneasily
as this enormous child,
its head bald as a giant mushroom,
reached out its pudgy hands
into every corner of its mother's life.

    The health visitor threw her graphs
    and charts into the sea.

The woman might have chosen
an infant made of leaves,
or one with lovely cloud formations
passing across his eyes.
Or one who fitted into a walnut shell.

    Stretched and torn,
    stitched, half-mended,
    she sighed and rested her head
    on her baby's broad chest.

The butterflies flew from her stomach,
and perched all over the bed.
How light they were,
how frail and buoyant!

Daddy Goes Hunting

What will Daddy bring back
when he goes hunting?

A woman from the forest
with red-berry lips?

Or perhaps he'll bring back
a rabbit skin –

fur softer than the thought of snow.
Dangerously soft, troubling fur.

He'll rub his bristly face against it
as he rubbed his cheek on our stomachs.

Draw his finger through it,
parting it like a harvester.

He'll not be happy to bring one skin –
he'll bring hundreds, and sew them together

with strong, rough stitches.
Pack the fridge with flesh,

awful and glassy.
Wrap us all in his blanket

until we're so hot we can hardly breathe.
Then we'll drift into sleep, pressing

our lips to tickling fur,
hold sweaty hands under the cover,

dig our chins into each other's chests.
In the morning we'll struggle free,

roll ourselves towards the walls,
while Daddy sets off for work,

banging our concealed front door,
scraping the ice off the windscreen.

Going hunting for a few hours, a few years.
Leaving us with his gunshot.

His promise to return.

Howls

No bricks. We've built our house with howls.
We've lain one howl upon another –
the wind helps us stick them together.

The wolf likes this house that's made of itself.
It crouches in the corner of the sitting-room,
mouth gaping, tongue red as a wound.

It assures us we lead strongly-scented lives.
We pick up each other's smell miles away,
hear each other's voice across the towns.

There's snow on the pine-fringed rug.
Snow on our eyebrows.
We are so very married, but the wolf

is fostering us as if we were its cubs.
His jaw closes on our backs,
leaves no scratch marks on our skin.

He's a surprisingly kind parent.
Plays tig. And tug-of-war.
Brings us bones to throw.

The Nest-Makers

I dreamt I saw the girls in the art room,
their long hair brushing the communal table.
They made wondrous nests in the northern light,
from fabric in spicy shades – coriander
with touches of chilli red and cardamom green –
fine cottons and velvets, torn into strips
and woven into bowls of twigs
and domes of grass. Nests not destined
for holes in trees or the crevices of buildings,
sailed on the table like small craft –
some already carrying their blue-white eggs.

The nest-makers. How to bring them back,
spy on them again, how to make a nest
in the brilliance of night.

In a Railway Carriage

We are alone in the carriage,
filling its narrowness.

He is so keen to hold my hand,
and I am so proud

that the King of Beasts
treats me as his friend.

He waves his paw
on the quiet side of my words,

has no need for lionesses,
spreading trees or reed beds.

Inclining his great head
with its serious mane,

he creates his own dusk.
This lion has singled me out

of the air.
We are contented,

leaning against each other.
The train stops at every station.

The world is too sleepy
to bang on the window.

Of Chairs and Shadows

(for Eileen Hogan)

When we tire of one another's conversation
it is such a relief

to let the chairs and shadows
take over in their unobtrusive way.

But they are not so quiet.
Chairs will converse with the walls,

the rugs, though chiefly
they're interested in their own shadows.

It's an uneasy relationship –
shadows are in love with themselves,

and so are chairs.
The shadow teases the chair mercilessly –

You are here. No, you were here.
I can help you to be more.

No, help you to be less.
Sometimes they do seem to speak in unison,

both daring to interrupt the light.
The chair boasts of its personality.

The shadow is neither impressed
nor unimpressed.

Shadows are beyond all this.
Both know when something momentous

is happening – could it be
the soul of a chair has been repaired?

Has there been a change in the room's
slow, bright, geometric dance?

What are shadows made of?
Ghosts, or smoke?

They throw their sharp,
their tender nets –

and we are caught like fish.